P.28

P.50

P.68

P.32

P.8

CONTENTS

Pedigree® Malcolm

Published 2011. Pedigree Books Ltd, Beech Hill House, Walnut Gardens, Exeter, Devon EX4 4DH
books@pedigreegroup.co.uk | www.pedigreebooks.com

£7.99

WHO'S THE CHAMP?

WWE CHAMPIONSHIP
1. The Miz

WORLD HEAVYWEIGHT CHAMPIONSHIP
3. Edge

UNITED STATES CHAMPIONSHIP
2. Sheamus

Can you work out who these six WWE Superstars are hidden behind the championship titles they have won in the past year.

Write their names in the blank spaces on the belts below. Then check your answers in the back!

DIVAS
4. EVE
CHAMPIONSHIP

TAG TEAM
6. heath slater +
justin gabriel
CHAMPIONSHIP

INTERCONTINENTAL
5. Kofi Kingston
CHAMPIONSHIP

EDGE

PROFILE

SMACK DOWN

Height:	6-foot-5
Weight:	250 pounds
From:	Toronto, Canada

Signature Move: Spear

Career Highlights:
WWE Champion;
World Heavyweight Champion;
World Tag Team Champion;
WWE Tag Team Champion;
Intercontinental Champion;
WCW U.S. Champion; 2001 King
of the Ring and Won first-ever
Money in the Bank Ladder Match

For the first time ever, *WrestleMania* opened with a world title match, which was eagerly anticipated by all 70,000 fans in Atlanta on the night.

Many had come to see whether Alberto Del Rio could continue the whirlwind start to his WWE career, which includes the *Royal Rumble* win that catapulted him into this *WrestleMania* showdown – a world title match he chose to participate in, and a decision which infuriated his opposite number.

In the opposing corner stood Edge who was aiming to

erase a blotch on his CV, namely the fact that he had never successfully defended a world title at *WrestleMania*.

Nine days before their epic dual, *SmackDown* General Manager Thoedore Long threw a snapper into the works by declaring that the 11-time world champion would have Christian in his corner – the celebrated tag team having recently been reunited after a decade apart – while supporting Del Rio would be his own partner in crime Brodus Clay.

With an already intense tag team rivalry giving the match added spice, there couldn't be a better way to get *WrestleMania XXVII* underway!

Height:	6-foot-5
Weight:	263 pounds
From:	San Luis Potosi, Mexico
Signature Move:	Cross armbreaker

Career Highlights:
Royal Rumble winner (2011)

"Del Rio enters the arena in his sparkling classic ride!"

"And here's Christian, who's supporting Edge!"

"Here comes the World Heavyweight Champion, with a world champion entrance!"

"Brodus Clay is in Alberto's corner tonight!"

"Edge starts by throwing a back body drop!"

"Alberto responds by putting the boot in!"

"Edge suffers a submission hold to his injured arm!"

"Del Rio fails with a flying dropkick and ends outside of the ring!"

"And Edge quickly follows..!"

"With a somersault dive over the top!"

"Back in the ring the world title fight is back on!"

"But Alberto maintains the upper hand!"

"And drills the champion with repeated punches!"

"Edge responds with an almighty boot to Del Rio!"

"He remains in control as they struggle to catch their breath!"

"Alberto goes for his fabled cross armbreaker!"

"Edge makes the ropes but Alberto hits an Enziguri. Wow!"

"Here's an arm bar submission by Alberto!"

"But Edge is a world champion for a reason!"

"Clay is here to help but Christian hits a DDT outside!"

"Edge saves his best until last and hits the spear!"

"And Del Rio is in a submission. It's all over!"

"He stays World Heavyweight Champion!"

· WORDSEARCH ·

He's the undisputed king of *WrestleMania*, but can you find the ten words listed below which are associated with the Undertaker and hidden in the wordsearch grid?

CHOKESLAM

WRESTLEMANIA

LASTOUTLAW

DEATH VALLEY

TOMBSTONE

BURIED ALIVE

PAUL BEARER

KANE

SHAWN MICHAELS

CASKET

I	A	I	N	A	M	E	L	T	S	E	R	W	N	H
M	R	O	E	X	J	G	N	W	J	D	E	A	T	H
Y	Q	E	F	P	V	C	A	P	L	D	P	E	V	B
D	E	A	T	H	V	A	L	L	E	Y	I	Q	B	U
X	V	J	W	G	R	E	D	M	C	I	D	T	R	R
V	R	E	J	P	G	N	J	K	W	R	N	O	H	I
C	F	J	H	I	T	A	P	R	U	U	S	M	E	E
A	G	E	V	Z	V	K	H	U	V	B	L	B	Q	D
S	L	E	A	H	C	I	M	N	W	A	H	S	R	A
K	D	T	Z	R	R	B	H	Z	I	W	X	T	S	L
E	E	P	J	A	Y	A	A	I	K	D	C	O	Z	I
T	L	R	E	R	A	E	B	L	U	A	P	N	P	V
W	A	L	T	U	O	T	S	A	L	T	L	E	H	E
M	A	L	S	E	K	O	H	C	H	G	D	X	M	N
S	Y	F	N	I	Q	W	I	G	U	S	M	A	M	V

CROSSWORD

Get to grips with Undertaker

You took on his mega wordsearch, now see if you can complete this Undertaker crossword using the clues about his fantastic career.

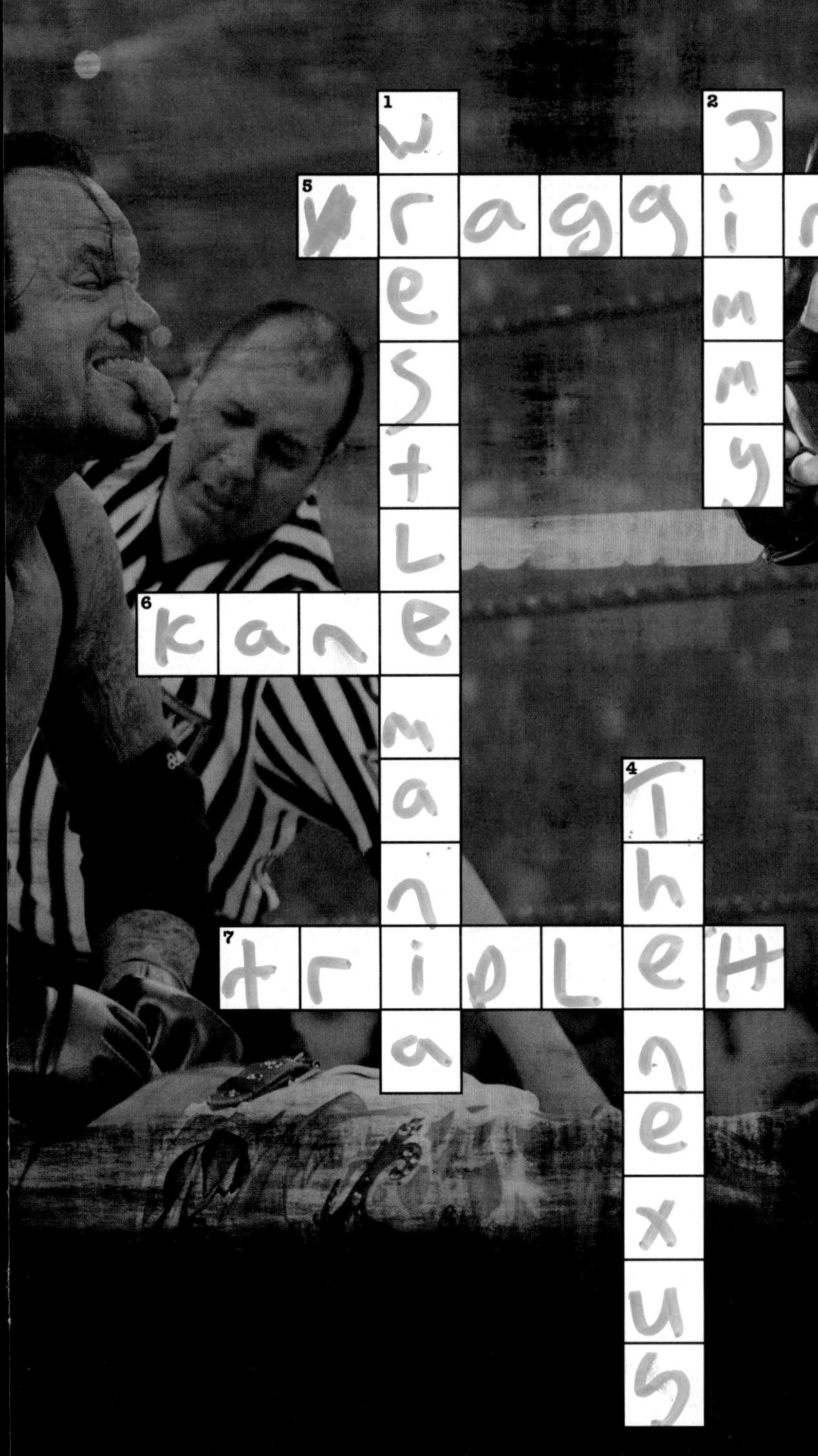

Down

1. He has a perfect 19/0 record on this, the greatest stage of them all.

2. ___ Snuka, his first *WrestleMania* victim in 1991

3. The _____ - Undertaker's nickname.

4. This group was involved in the rivalry between Undertaker and Kane.

Across

5. He took part in a Buried Alive match at this pay-per-view event.

6. His brother in WWE.

7. Opponent at *WrestleMania XXVII.*

Q1 Can you unravel the fridge magnet letters to reveal an original member of The Nexus

SLATHERA HT

Heath slater

10 pts

Q2 The group debuted on the Viewers Choice edition of *Raw*, during the main event match between John Cena and who?

a. CM Punk ✓

b. John Morrison

c. Ted DiBiase

d. Sheamus

10 pts

Q3 The Newcomer

Can you work out the name of the latest member of The Nexus?

MASON RYAN

10 pts

Q4 Fly the flag

Which of these flags is the homeland of Justin Gabriel?

a. Italian flag

b. South African flag ✓

c. GB flag

d. Spanish flag

10 pts

Q5 David Otunga and John Cena won The Nexus' first titles in which pay-per-view event in 2010?

a. Hell in a Cell

b. SummerSlam

c. Extreme Rules

d. Bragging Rights

10 pts

How much do you know about The Nexus? Take our tough-tackling quiz – there's 10 points available for each correct answer, so see if you can get the magical 130-point mark!

Your score: **???** out of 130 points

Q6 — Complete the name of CM Punks entrance music

This Fire ....*Burns*........

- a. Hurts ☐
- b. Burns ☑
- c. Sweats ☐
- d. Scalds ☐

10 pts

Q7 — True or False?

a. Michael McGillicutty & CM Punk challenged Santino Marella & Vladimir Kozlov for the WWE Tag Team Championship **T** **F**

b. Skip Sheffield was actually born in Sheffield, England **T** **F**

a. = 10 pts & b = 10pts

Q8

Who is it?

Mason Ryan

10 pts

Q9 — The official New Nexus motto under CM Punk is what?

- a. Faith ☑
- b. Forward ☐
- c. Fortune ☐
- d. Fearsome ☐

10 pts

Q10 — Name the dudes

These three members of The Nexus have their faces blanked out, but can you work out who they are?

a. *H. Harris*

b. *D. Otunga*

c. *CM Punk*

10pts Each

NEW TO THE GAME

These Superstars are new to the WWE Universe but can they talk the talk as well as walk the walk?

Can you match up each statement to the correct Superstar?

⑧ ⑤ ⑥ ④ ①

⑦ ② ③

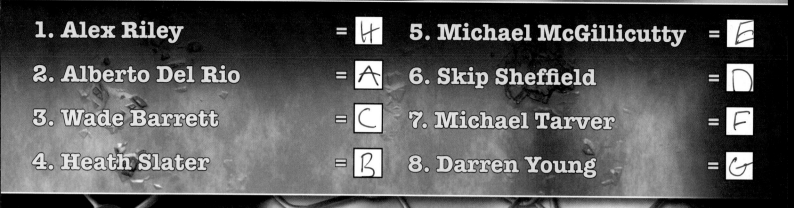

1. Alex Riley = H
2. Alberto Del Rio = A
3. Wade Barrett = C
4. Heath Slater = B

5. Michael McGillicutty = E
6. Skip Sheffield = D
7. Michael Tarver = F
8. Darren Young = G

A. "Thirty-nine men couldn't beat me. I am the *Royal Rumble king*"

B. "The misspelling of The Corre is all down to me!"

C. "Forget The Nexus – leading The Corre is where it's at!"

D. "A broken ankle might keep me down, but I'll be back!"

E. "I aim to be 'Perfect' like my father Curt Hennig!"

F. "Wade Barrett discarded me from The Nexus, but The Panther will pounce again!"

G. "With help from Chavo Guerrero, I've got NXT Redemption!"

H. "I am the apprentice of The Miz – John Cena has nothing on me!"

HITTING TOP GEAR!

1. A.D.R ? ? ? ? ? ? ?

2. ? Sheamus ? ?

3. John Cena ? ? ?

4. Jerry ? ? ? ?

22

5. undertaker ? ? ?

6. drewmcintire ? ? ?

7. hamswoggle ? ? ?

8. The big show ? ? ?

WHAT DO YOU KNOW?

In profile...

Look at these WWE profile cards. See if you can fill in the missing gaps from the mixture of answers provided.

Missing Words

Mexico
Starship
Seven
Spear
~~Riley~~
Heavyweight
~~Klutch~~

CM PUNK®

Height:	6-foot-1
Weight:	222 pounds
From:	Chicago, IL
Signature Move:	Go To Sleep, Koji _Klutch_

Career Highlights:
World Heavyweight Champion; World Tag Team Champion

Associates: The New Nexus

JOHN MORRISON®

Height:	6-foot-1
Weight:	223 pounds
From:	Los Angeles, CA
WWE Debut:	2005
Signature Move:	_Starship_ Pain, & The Moonlight Drive

Career Highlights:
Intercontinental Champion; WWE Tag Team Champion

THE MIZ®

Height:	6-foot-1
Weight:	231 pounds
From:	Cleveland, OH
Signature Move:	Skull-Crushing Finale

Career Highlights:
WWE Champion; WWE Tag Team Champion; World Tag Team Champion

Associates: Alex _Riley_

ALBERTO DEL RIO™

Height: 6-foot-5

Weight: 263 pounds

From: San Luis Potosi, Mexico

Signature Move: Cross Armbreaker

Career Highlights:
Royal Rumble winner 2011

BIG SHOW®

Height: seven foot

Weight: 485 pounds

From: Tampa, FL

Signature Moves: Chokeslam, & Cobra Clutch Backbreaker

Career Highlights:
WWE Champion; World Tag Team Champion; WWE Hardcore Champion; Unified WWE Tag Team Champion

EDGE®

Height: 6-foot-5

Weight: 241 pounds

From: Toronto, Canada

Signature Move: Spear

Career Highlights:
WWE Champion; World Heavyweight Champion; World Tag Team Champion; WWE Tag Team Champion; Unified Tag Team Champion

JOHN CENA®

Height: 6-foot-1

Weight: 240 pounds

From: West Newbury, MA

Signature Moves: Attitude Adjustment, STF

Career Highlights:
World Heavyweight Champion; WWE Champion; World Tag Team Champion; WWE Tag Team Champion; 2008 *Royal Rumble* Winner

WHAT DO YOU KNOW?

In profile...

Look at these WWE profile cards. See if you can fill in the missing gaps from the mixture of answers provided.

Missing Words   Killswitch

Paul   Dublin

Valley   Strongest

WrestleMania   India

MARK HENRY®

Height:	6-foot-1
Weight:	392 pounds
From:	Silsbee, TX
Signature Moves:	World's Strongest Slam
Career Highlights:	
ECW Champion; European Champion	
Associate:	Evan Bourne

SHEAMUS®

Height:	6-foot-6
Weight:	272 pounds
From:	Dublin, Ireland
Signature Moves:	High Cross, Brogue Kick, Irish Curse
Career Highlights:	
WWE Champion; U.S. Champion; 2010 King of the Ring	

THE GREAT KHALI®

Height:	7-foot-3
Weight:	420 pounds
From:	India
Career Highlights:	
World Heavyweight Champion	
Associate:	Ranjin Singh

CHRISTIAN®

Height: 6-foot-2

Weight: 227 pounds

From: Toronto, Canada

Signature Move: *Killswitch*

Career Highlights:
World Heavyweight Champion; Intercontinental Champion; World Tag Team Champion; Hardcore Champion; European Champion

Associate: Ron Hutchinson

KANE®

Height: 7-foot

Weight: 323 pounds

From: Knoxville, TN

Signature Move: Chokeslam

Career Highlights:
WWE Champion; World Heavyweight Champion; World Tag Team Champion; Hardcore Champion

Associate: *Paul* Bearer

UNDERTAKER®

Height: 6-foot-7

Weight: 299 pounds

From: Death *Valley*

Signature Moves: Chokeslam; Tombstone; & Last Ride

Career Highlights:
WWE Champion; World Heavyweight Champion; World Tag Team Champion; Hardcore Champion; undefeated at *WrestleMania* (19-0)

REY MYSTERIO®

Height: 5-foot-6

Weight: 175 pounds

From: San Diego, CA

Signature Moves: 619; West Coast Pop

Career Highlights:
World Heavyweight Championship *WrestleMania* 22, 2006); Royal Rumble winner 2006; WWE Tag Team Champion; Intercontinental Champion

REY MYSTERIO® **VS** **CODY RHODES™**

RAW | SMACK DOWN

There was no bigger rivalry going into *WrestleMania XXVII* than Rhodes versus Mysterio. Back in January, Rey accidentally broke Cody's nose in a *SmackDown* match while performing the 619, leaving the former

'Dashing' one needing surgery and unable to compete at *Elimination Chamber* or the *Royal Rumble*. There was only one way he was going to settle this: inside the squared circle, on the biggest stage of all…

"Introducing Cody Rhodes, his mask hiding his self-proclaimed disfigurement!"

"He blames his arch rival Rey Mysterio, and here he is!"

"Mysterio starts off with a flying hurricanrana from the top rope!"

"But Rhodes quickly recovers – and we see a smile behind the mask!"

"Rey receives his own blow to the face. That's gotta hurt!"

"Surely Cody can't reveal what's behind Rey's famed mask!"

"Wow, look at this – Rey is being held in a suplex!"

"He's landing the superplex more like!"

"But Rey's recovered in his own spectacular style!"

"More pain for Rey – this is a match too close to call!"

"He's down but what is Cody thinking?"

"Look, he's exposing the knee brace that has caused him so much damage!"

"But after the controversy Rey responds with a Moonsault!"

"Watch him come in for a smooth landing!"

"Rey's taken off Cody's mask and parades it like a badge of honour!"

"He then unleashes a 619!"

"You can almost taste the impact!"

"He then goes for a Splash from the top rope!"

"Unmasked, Cody appears a beaten man. Another blow rains in!"

"He's now rolled outside the ring to buy himself some time!"

"But Rhodes has one last trick up his sleeve. He's stuck Rey with the brace!"

"And that's it! Rey is out! There's no coming back! Cody has his revenge!"

VS

RAW

SMACK DOWN

Ever since the New Nexus attacked Randy Orton, there has been a real air of tension between The Viper and CM Punk - the New Nexus leader. Orton had managed to take out every other member of the group, except The Second City Saviour, who used a tour bus and Orton's family members to badly injure his knee. A week later, Punk then left his big rival unconscious following a GTS and at *WrestleMania* was out to unleash more pain. Still injured, The Viper was on the back foot, but could he exact revenge in front of the millions…

"He might be missing the New Nexus but CM Punk looks ready for business!"

"You've gotta fancy his chances given Orton's knee injury!"

"Punk wastes no time attacking that knee!"

"He also goes for the GTS but Randy wriggles free.."

"The Viper bites back with a clothes line…"

"… which leaves Punk heading straight for the canvas!"

"A powerslam then leaves Punk facing a two count!"

"A DDT leaves Orton stomping the canvas!"

"Orton prepares for the RKO but Punk slides out!"

"But incredibly the Viper turns the move mid-air into an RKO!"

"He then attempts to launch Randy from the top rope!"

"He then goes for the pin. The Second City Saviour is out for good!"

"We have just witnessed The Viper at his best!"

EIGHT MAN TAG TEAM

WrestleMania wouldn't be the same without a tag team match to light up the ring. This year was no different as Kane, Big Show, Santino Marella and Kofi Kingston took on the might of Wade Barrett, Ezekiel Jackson, Heath Slater and Justin Gabriel - aka 'The Corre'. Use your pens or pencils to colour in the eight-man madness!

MIND THE GAPS

WrestleMania XXVII was an event like no other! See what you can remember from the star-studded night by filling in the gaps below.

WrestleMania XXVII was held at the  Dome in Atlanta.

The Undertaker came into the event hoping to take his undefeated streak to [19] /0.

He took part in a No [holds] Barred match against Triple H.

The [Rock] appeared on the night as the host.

Steve [Austin] was the guest referee for the match between Michael Cole and Jerry Lawler.

A six-person mixed tag team match featured Stratus.

Cody Rhodes came out to face Rey Mysterio wearing a [Mask].

Randy Orton faced CM Punk with an injured .

Missing words: Holds, Trish, Knee, Rock, Austin, 19, Georgia, Mask.

SPOT THE DIFFERENCE

Take a look at this World Heavyweight Championship match between Edge and Alberto Del Rio at *WrestleMania XXVII* and see if you can spot the ten differences.

39

HALL OF MIRRORS

1. Triple H ? ? ? ?

2. The Miz ? ? ?

5. ?big show ? ? ?

6. ?rey mysterio ?

These WWE Superstars have gone to the fair and entered the crazy Hall of Mirrors. Can you work out who they are?

Write their names in the blank spaces, Then check your answers on page 77.

3. JohnMorrison

4. The great Khali

7. Undertaker

8. hornswiggle

THE ULTIMATE RAW QUIZ

Q1
Hair Raising!

What's gone wrong with Dolph Ziggler? Look at these three pictures of him and work out whose hair he's wearing.

a. *R truth*   b. *Zyder*   c. *J morrison*

a. = 10 pts, b = 10pts & c = 10pts

Q2
In the 2010 King of the Ring competition, Sheamus beat who in the final?

a. Daniel Bryan
b. Ezekiel Jackson
c. John Cena
d. John Morrison ✓

10pts

Q3
All washed up

Look inside the washine machine. Can you work out which superstar has been washing his clothes?

J cena

10pts

Q4
Nickname know-how

Jerry Lawler is also known as...

a. The Special One
b. The Prince
c. The King ✓
d. The Legend

10pts

Q5
Big Country

Which country do you associate with Santino Marella?

a. USA
b. Italy ✓
c. France
d. India

10pts

42

...FACTS. TRIVIA. NEWS AND PROFILES...FACTS. TRIVIA. NEWS AND PROFILES...FACTS. TRIVIA. NEWS AND PROFILES...FACTS. TRIVIA. NEWS

...AND PROFILES...FACTS. TRIVIA. NEWS AND PROFILES...FACTS. TRIVIA. NEWS AND PROFILES...FACTS. TRIVIA. NEWS AND PROFILES...FACTS. TRIVIA. NEWS AND PROFILES...FACTS. TRIVIA. NEWS AND PROFILES...FACTS. TRIVIA. NEWS AND PROFILES...FACTS. TRIVIA. NEWS AND PRO

How much do you know about *Raw*? Take our tough-tackling quiz – there's 10 points available for each correct answer, so see if you can get the 150-points!

RAW

Your score: ??? **out of 150 points**

...FACTS. TRIVIA. NEWS AND PROFILES...FACTS. TRIVIA. NEWS AND PROFILES...FACTS. TRIVIA. NEWS AND PROFILES...FACTS. TRIVIA. NEWS

...AND PROFILES...FACTS. TRIVIA. NEWS AND PROFILES...FACTS. TRIVIA. NEWS AND PROFILES...FACTS. TRIVIA. NEWS AND PROFILES...FACTS. TRIVIA. NEWS AND PROFILES...FACTS. TRIVIA. NEWS AND PRO

Q6

Milestone magic

Raw celebrated what milestone episode last August?

a. 300th episode ☐
b. 600th episode ☐
c. 900th episode ☑
d. 1,000th episode ☐

10pts

Q7

True or false?

Michael Cole and Jerry Lawler are the current *Raw* commentators?

True ✓ | False

10pts

Q8

Guess who?
Look at this pixelated image of a *Raw* superstar. Can you work out who it is?

Goldust

10pts

Q9

The Legend

Can you name this legendary *Raw* superstar?

H I P L E T R

Triple H

10pts

Q10

Mini wordsearch

Can you find these *Raw* superstars? Ten points for each...

Primo ☑ Eve ☑ The Miz ☑ Tamina ☑

A	A	K	J	P	Z
B	N	M	R	S	I
T	I	I	O	N	M
A	M	T	U	B	E
O	A	E	V	E	H
A	T	P	O	T	T

10pts Each

43

LADDERS MATCH-UP

These Superstars have all featured in Ladder Matches but can you re-arrange the letters to match up the superstar with the correct ladder?

Write their names in the blank spaces, check your answers in the back!

1 John Morrison

2 Dolph Ziggler

3 Christian

4 Jack Swagger

5 Sheamus

6 Kofi Kingston

45

THE ROCK

..."IF YA SMEELLLL WHAT THE ROCK IS COOKIN'!!"

…IS BACK!!!

Anaheim, California was the scene. February 14, 2011 was the day, the day that the members of WWE Universe erupted in ovation like never before when The Rock's music hit and "The Great One" made his way to the ring. After a seven year absence "The People's Champ" grabbed the microphone and proved exactly why he is "The Most Electrifying Man in all of Entertainment", by electrifying and entertaining the "Millions and Millions" of Rock's fans as only he can. The Rock has called his Raw return, "the greatest Raw moment I have ever had in my entire career".

That statement speaks volumes coming from a man who made his way through the best that WWE had to offer from his beginnings as Rocky Maivia to his epic battles with Stone Cold Steve Austin on the Grandest Stage of them all, WrestleMania. The Rock has done it all – trail-blazing, eyebrow-raising, jabroni-beating and pie-eating the whole way through, and if you didn't like it, then The Rock drove you straight down Jabroni Drive and checked you right into the SmackDown hotel!

So...you think you know everything about The Rock? IT DOESN'T MATTER WHAT YOU THINK!! So know your role, shut your mouth, and check out these cool trivia facts about this true WWE icon.

The world was introduced to The Rock in May of 1972. The future People's Champ was born in Hayward, California and given his full name, Dwayne Johnson.

A third-generation Superstar, The Rock had WWE in his blood from the very beginning. His father Rocky Johnson was a groundbreaking Superstar who made history with partner Tony Altas by becoming the first black tag team to win the World Tag Team Championship. His grandfather, High Chief Peter Maivia, was also a Superstar and was the patriarch of the entire Samoan wrestling family.

Before bringing his talents to the WWE Universe, Dwayne Johnson electrified the American football gridiron as a member of the Miami Hurricanes National Championship team. As #94 on the defensive side of the ball, opponents felt the early developments of the Rock Bottom finisher begin to take shape.

When he burst onto the scene in 1996, it did not take young Rocky Maivia long to make an impact. He became the sole survivor at Survivor Series and would soon take home the Intercontinental Championship.

Still not quite the People's Champ, he joined the villainous Nation of Domination in 1997. It was during his

time in the nation that he began raising his trademark "People's Eyebrow".

The Rock became WWE Champion just two years into his WWE career and went on to win the coveted title an astonishing 7 times! He also holds 2 Intercontinental Title reigns, 5 Tag Team Championships, and a Royal Rumble Match victory (2000) to his credit.

At WrestleMania XIX, The Rock and Stone Cold Steve Austin clashed on the grandest stage for an unprecedented third time! Over the years, The Rock has always brought it to WrestleMania. His Legend vs. Icon Match against Hulk Hogan at WrestleMania X8 lived up to the billing as one of the most epic battles of all time.

Aside from sports entertainment, The Rock has achieved mainstream status as one of the hottest commodities on the silver screen. His movie credits include The Mummy Returns, The Scorpion King, Walking Tall, The Game Plan, Race to Witch Mountain and Fast Five.

In March 2008, he had the honor of inducting his father and grandfather into the WWE Hall of Fame. His match against John Cena at WrestleMania XXVIII will be the most anticipated WrestleMania main event of all time, and you can rest assured that John Cena, the WWE Universe and the "Millions and Millions" of Rock's fans around the world will SMELL WHAT THE ROCK IS COOKIN'!

HOW TO DRAW THE MIZ

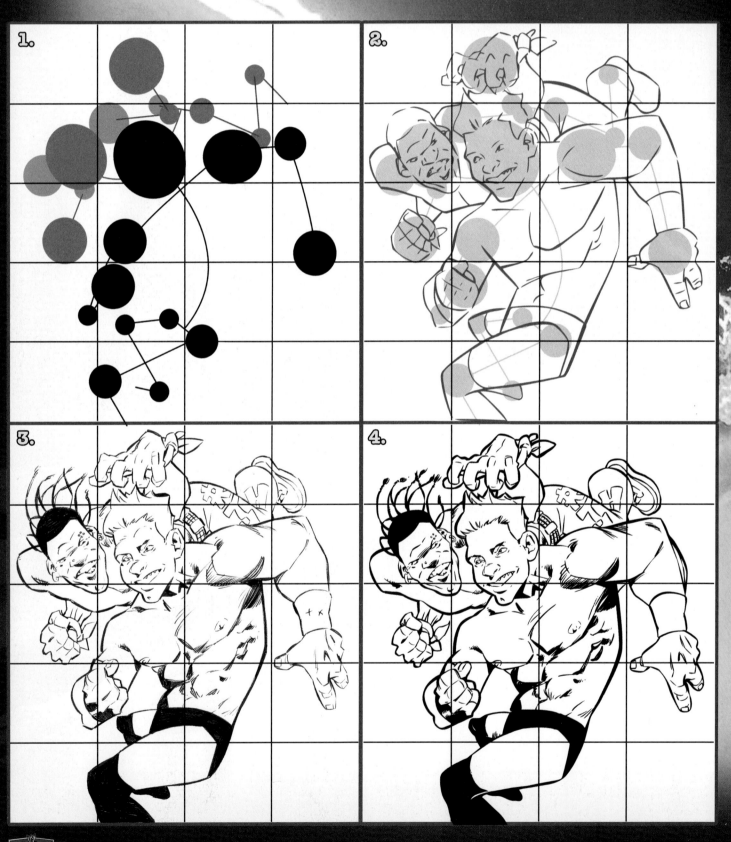

Take a look at this picture of The Miz taking on R-Truth during 2010's Fatal 4-Way event and see if you can copy with a sketch of your own. Follow our simple steps and it's easy!

1. Draw pencil lines to get the positions of the The Miz and R-Truth's bodies.
2. Now lightly sketch in both fighters outlines.
3. Fill in more details, add some colours and shadings.
4. Complete your drawing by outlining it with a nice thick black pen.

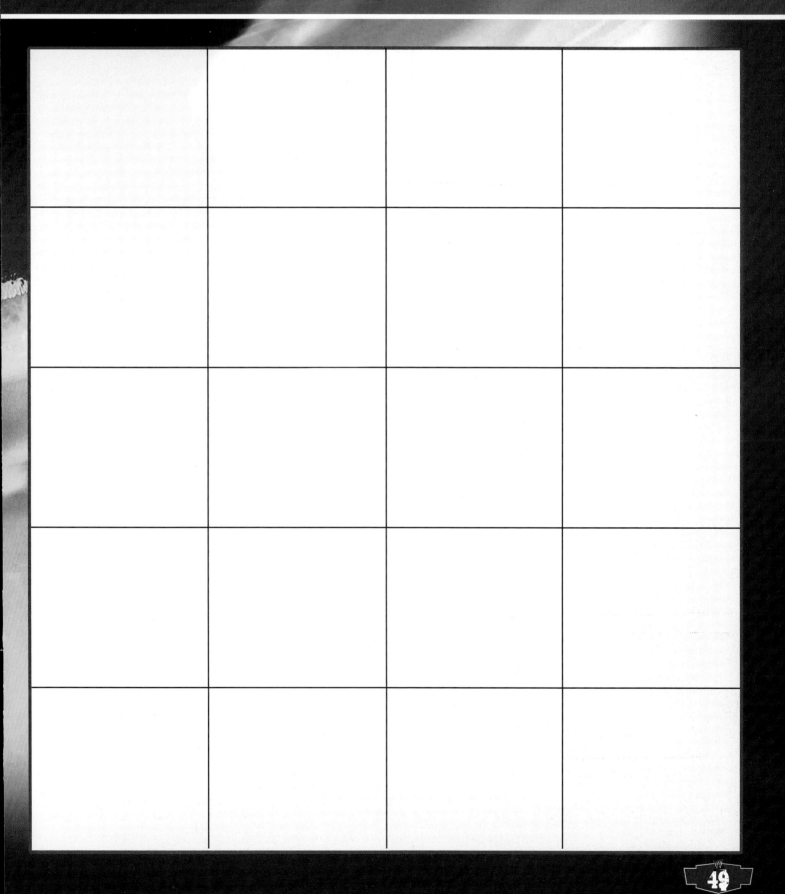

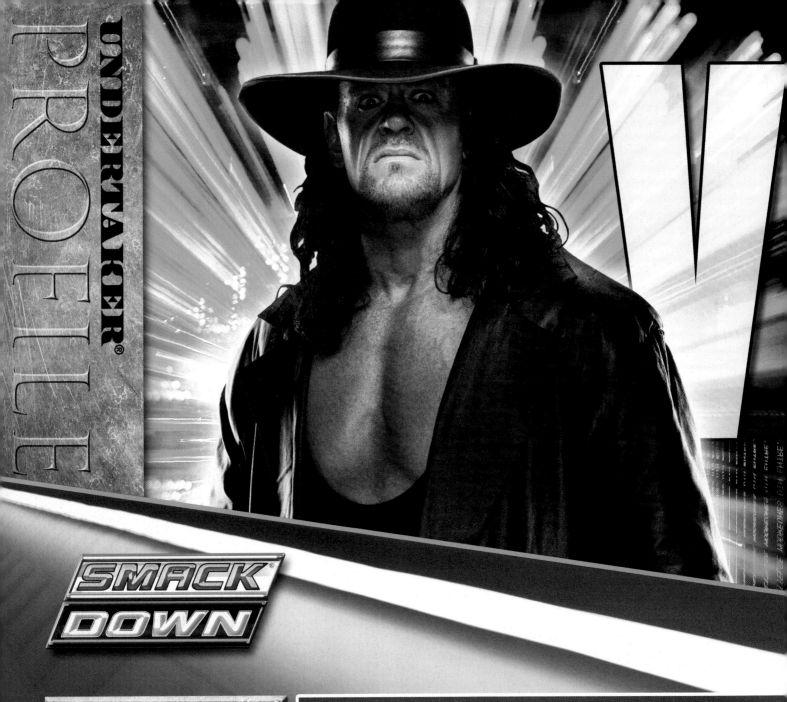

SMACK DOWN

Height: 6-foot-10

Weight: 299 pounds

From: Death Valley

Signature Move: Chokeslam; Tombstone; Last Ride

Career Highlights:
WWE Champion;
World Heavyweight Champion;
World Tag Team Champion;
WCW Tag Team Champion;
Hardcore Champion;
Undefeated *WrestleMania* champion

Triple H headed to *WrestleMania XXVII* hoping to achieve what no other Superstar has achieved before – namely defeating Undertaker on The Grandest Stage of Them All...

This was billed as a true clash of the giants. Both men are already assured of a place in WWE folklore, but while they have both enjoyed and endured plenty of success down the years, The Deadman has always had the upper hand over his opposite and, indeed, everyone else in the WWE Universe – namely his 18/0 record at *WrestleMania*.

S

RAW

Now Triple H would get the chance to put a blemish on Undertaker's proud record. This 'No Holds Barred' match came to light when The Phenom's return to the ring earlier in the year was interrupted by The King of Kings. There was no war of words at the time, no physical encounter, just a stare that said, 'let's get it on at *WrestleMania!*'

And so the time had arrived. The Game now had his one big chance, to go where the likes of Ric Flair, Kane, Edge and Shawn Michaels have all tried and failed – to beat The Deadman and take his own place in *WrestleMania* history…

Height:	6-foot-4
Weight:	255 pounds
From:	Greenwich, CT
Signature Move:	Pedigree

Career Highlights:
WWE Champion;
World Heavyweight Champion;
Intercontinental Champion;
Unified WWE Tag Team Champion;
World Tag Team Champion;
European Champion;
King of the Ring (1997);
Royal Rumble winner (2002)

"The lights are dimmed and Triple H enters the arena!"

"Undertaker enters to a sea of fog!"

"It's face off time for these *WrestleMania* greats!"

"Undertaker is nailed with several right hands!"

"Ouch! Undertaker is thrown into the ringside barrier!"

"Triple suffers a back body drop off the table!"

"But hits back with a spinebuster through the Spanish Table!"

"Undertaker surprises Triple H with a chokeslam back in the ring!"

"And he is on his way down to a two-count!"

"Triple H recovers to unleash some serious punishment!"

"He rains down a number of blows in the corner!"

"But look, The Deadman has turned it into The Last Ride!"

"Triple H is heading for another mighty fall!"

"This match is in the balance. Triple H has thrown another spinebuster!"

"Now he's brought a steel chair into the ring!"

"And is attacking Undertaker with it!"

"But 'Taker let's fly and the chair hits Triple H in the head!"

"He replies with a pedigree! One…two… 'Taker is up in time!"

"Undertaker hits a tombstone – it's another two-count!"

"Then Triple H replies with a tombstone of his own!"

"And then grabs his trusty sledgehammer from under the ring!"

"But before he can use it, 'Taker has him in Hell's Gate! It's submission time!"

"19 and 0 says it all. Undertaker's a *WrestleMania* legend!"

OLD SCHOOL WHO?

1. _Jim duggen_

Known by his nickname 'Hacksaw', you might remember this Hall of Famer appearing in the 2009 *Royal Rumble* match, where he was eliminated by Big Show.

STAT ATTACK

Height: 6-foot-3

Signature move: Three Point Stance Clothesline

Highlights:
United States Champion; winner of the first-ever *Royal Rumble* in 1988.

Debut: 1987

2. _Mr perfect_

Also known as Curt Hennig, this Hall of Famer was also the longest-reigning Intercontinental champion of the 1990s. He is the father to current WWE Superstar Michael McGillicutty and son of Larry 'The Axe' Hennig.

STAT ATTACK

Height: 6-foot-3

Signature move: Atomic drop

Highlights:
Intercontinental Championship; Hall of Fame (Class of 2007).

Debut: 1982

3. _british butldog_

Partnered in the ring alongside the Dynamite Kid, he hailed from England and enjoyed four successful spells in WWE. Sadly, he died in 2002 aged just 39.

STAT ATTACK

Height: 6-foot-1

Signature move: Armdrag, Crucifix, Running powerbomb

Highlights: European Championship; World Tag Team Championship.

Debut: 1979

When Raw went 'Old School' for one night only with a host of former Superstars entering the fray there were some nostalgic blasts from the past. But can you name these WWE legends?

4. Stone cold Steve austin

A three-time *Royal Rumble* winner, he was forced to retire due to injury in 2003. He returned to host the TV reality series Tough Enough.

STAT ATTACK

Height: 6-foot-2

Signature move: Stone Cold Stunner

Highlights: WWE Champion; World Tag Team Champion; King of the Ring (1996); *Royal Rumble* (1997, 1998, 2001).

Debut: 1995

5. Shawn michaels

Debut as a member of The Rockers, he is a three-time WWE Champion, and retired after losing to Undertaker at *WrestleMania XXVI*.

STAT ATTACK

Height: 6-foot-1

Signature move: Sweet Chin Music

Highlights: WWE Champion; World Heavyweight Champion; World Tag Team Champion; *Royal Rumble* (1995, 1996)

Debut: 1988

6. booker T

This six-time World Champion from Houston returned to WWE in 2011 as part of the Royal Rumble. He's now part of the SmackDown commentating team.

STAT ATTACK

Height: 6-foot-3

Signature move: Axe Kick

Highlights: World Heavyweight Champion; World Tag Team Champion; Intercontinental Champion; United States Champion; Hardcore Champion; King of the Ring (2006).

Debut: 2001

THE ULTIMATE SMACKDOWN QUIZ

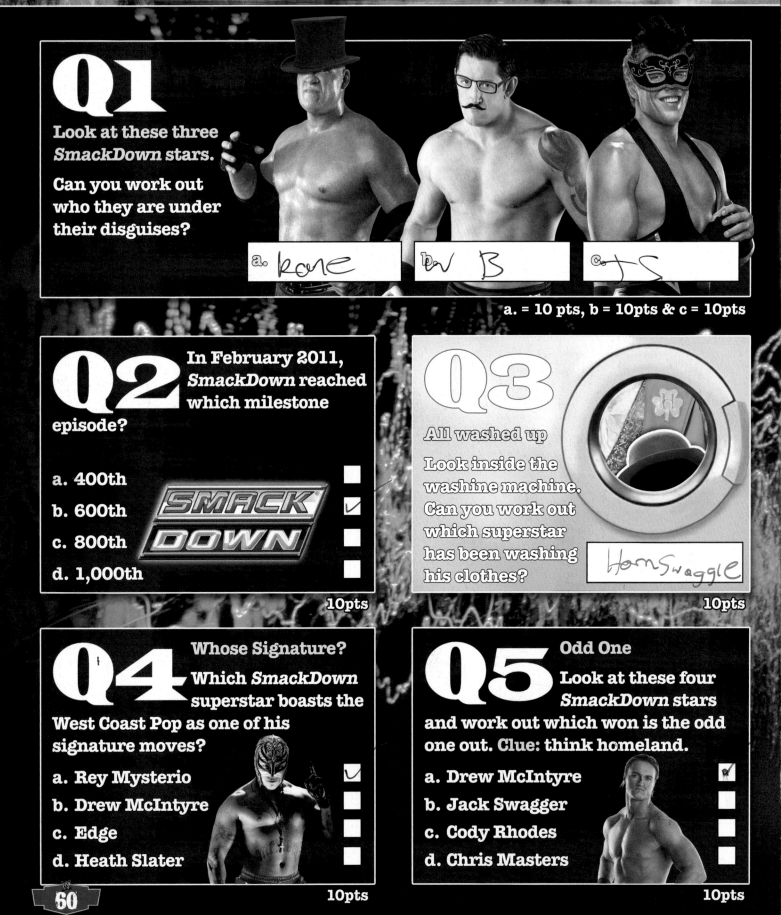

Q1

Look at these three *SmackDown* stars.

Can you work out who they are under their disguises?

a. *kane*

b. *B*

c. *JS*

a. = 10 pts, b = 10pts & c = 10pts

Q2

In February 2011, *SmackDown* reached which milestone episode?

a. 400th
b. 600th ✓
c. 800th
d. 1,000th

10pts

Q3

All washed up

Look inside the washine machine. Can you work out which superstar has been washing his clothes?

HornSwoggle

10pts

Q4

Whose Signature?

Which *SmackDown* superstar boasts the West Coast Pop as one of his signature moves?

a. Rey Mysterio ✓
b. Drew McIntyre
c. Edge
d. Heath Slater

10pts

Q5

Odd One

Look at these four *SmackDown* stars and work out which won is the odd one out. Clue: think homeland.

a. Drew McIntyre ✓
b. Jack Swagger
c. Cody Rhodes
d. Chris Masters

10pts

FACTS TRIVIA NEWS AND PROFILES FACTS TRIVIA NEWS AND PROFILES FACTS TRIVIA NEWS AND PROFILES FACTS TRIVIA NEWS AND PROFILES FACTS TRIVIA NEWS AND PROFILES FACTS TRIVIA NEWS AND PROFILES FACTS TRIVIA NEWS AND PROFILES FACTS TRIVIA NEWS AND PROFILES FACTS TRIVIA NEWS AND PROFILES FACTS TRIVIA NEWS AND PROFILES FACTS TRIVIA NEWS AND PROFILES FACTS TRIVIA NEWS AND PROFILES FACTS TRIVIA NEWS AND PROFILES FACTS TRIVIA NEWS AND PROFILES FACTS TRIVIA NEWS AND PROFILES FACTS TRIVIA NEWS AND PROFILES FACTS TRIVIA NEWS AND PRO

How much do you know about *SmackDown*? Take our tough-tackling quiz – there's ten points available for each correct answer. See if you can get the magical 170 point mark!

SMACK DOWN

Your score: [???] out of 170 points

FACTS TRIVIA NEWS AND PROFILES FACTS TRIVIA NEWS AND PROFILES FACTS TRIVIA NEWS AND PROFILES FACTS TRIVIA NEW VIA NEWS AND PROFILES FACTS TRIVIA NEWS AND PROFILES FACTS TRIVIA PROFILES FACTS TRIVIA NEWS AND PROFILES FACTS TRIVIA NEWS AND PROFILES FACTS TRIVIA NEWS AND PROFILES FACTS TRIVIA NEWS AND PROFILES FACTS TRIVIA NEWS AND PROFILES FACTS TRIVIA NEWS AND PRO

Q6 Up in lights

Can you work out which Superstar has his name up in lights on the billboard?

S A N C H I T I R

Christian

10pts

Q7

True or false?

Cody Rhodes' father is Hacksaw Jim Duggan?

[True] [✓ False]

10pts

Q8

Guess who?
Look at this pixelated image. Can you work out who the Superstar is?

Kofi kingsto

10pts

Q9 What's missing

Can you fill in these missing words associated with Alberto Del Rio? Ten points for each...

Alberto comes from the country of *Mexico*. He made his *SmackDown* debut in the year *2010*. He won the 2011 *Royal Rumble* by last eliminating *Santino*.

10pts Each

Q10

Mini wordsearch

Can you find these *SmackDown* superstars? Ten points for each...

Edge ✓ JTG ✓ Layla ✓ Kane ✓

Q	R	T	R	J	A
B	N	H	F	T	G
E	E	P	R	G	A
G	N	P	A	U	L
D	A	L	Y	A	L
E	K	S	G	I	B

10pts Each

MANIC MAZE

HUSKY HARRIS

TED DIBIASE

KANE

ALICIA FOX

It's that time in the year when our **WWE** Superstars are already looking ahead to *WrestleMania XXVIII* in Miami and you must work out the maze to see who can get there first.

WADE BARRETT

CODY RHODES

DAVID OTUNGA

BETH PHOENIX

WHO SHOULDN'T BE THERE?

Group 1

Santino Marella   John Cena   Sheamus   Drew McIntyre

Group 2

Michael Cole   Jerry Lawler   Booker T   Theodore Long

Look at these four groups of WWE Superstars. Study each one closely and try to work out who is the odd one out in each box...

Group 1 = No one

Group 2 = No one

Group 3 = christian

Group 4 = No one

Group 3

| Kane | Dolph Ziggler | Edge | Wade Barrett |

Group 4

| Big Show (485lb) | The Great Khali (420lb) | Kane (323 lbs) | Mark Henry (418 lbs) |

Undertaker

Undertaker

RULES!

He's got the most prolific record in *WrestleMania* history, so it's time to take a trip down memory lane and remember some of the Undertaker's finest performances on the grandest stage of all.

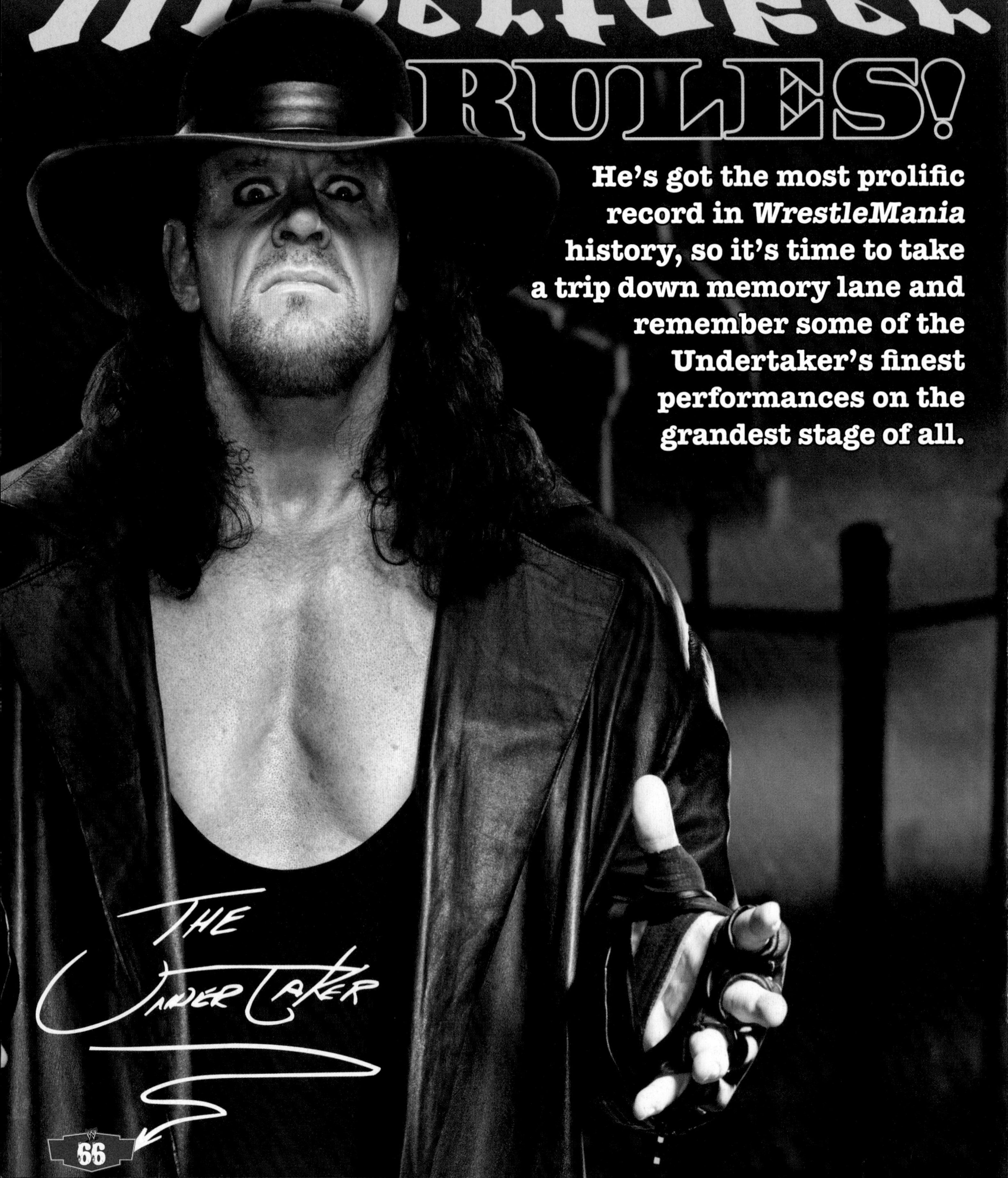

THE Undertaker

Undertaker v Shawn Michaels

With both men on a hot streak in terms of *WrestleMania* matches, the crowd was at fever pitch as Michaels entered the arena in white, followed by Undertaker in his trademark black. Coming from opposite ends of the spectrum, the match had the fans split but they were all in agreement that the awesome displays put on by both superstars were up there with the best ever. Signature moves were the name of the game and it was a fearsome Tombstone Piledriver that finally finished off Michaels.

Undertaker v Shawn Michaels

WRESTLEMANIA XXVI

Billed as a 'Streak v Career' match, the pair resumed their immense rivalry and it was the Tombstone Piledriver that again put paid to Michaels. A third Tombstone of the night ended with Michaels pinned and his illustrious career finally brought to an end. Undertaker, meanwhile, took his *WrestleMania* record to 18-0, and after the match the pair shook hands and embraced.

Undertaker v Batista

WRESTLEMANIA 23

Defending the World Heavyweight Championship, Batista flew out of the blocks with a spear before Undertaker thought he'd had the match won with a fearsome Chokeslam. Somehow, Batista kicked out as the stakes were raised even higher. 'The Animal' managed to perform a powerslam on Undertaker outside of the ring before a match-winning Tombstone Piledriver was unleashed – the 'Phenom' becoming the first superstar to win both the World Heavyweight Championship and the WWE Championship at *WrestleMania*.

Undertaker v Triple H

WRESTLEMANIA X-SEVEN

The match started with the two superstars fighting outside of the ring, then referee Mike Chioda was knocked out by Undertaker, who became vexed over a two-count. Another brawl outside of the ring took place but once Chioda regained consciousness, order was finally restored. Triple H then took the upper hand with a number of blows to the head, before Undertaker reversed them with the Last Ride, followed by a pin, to take his winning streak at *WrestleMania* to 9/0.

Undertaker v Jimmy Snuka

WRESTLEMANIA VII

This event marked Undertaker's *WrestleMania* debut and it came just five months after he first set foot in the WWE universe. He might have been a relative unknown but he grabbed everyone's attention as he swatted 'Superfly' Jimmy Snuka in a one-sided match. It was a contest which also saw the Tombstone Piledriver come to the fore for the first time. As a contest, well, it was a no contest and lasted just four minutes and 20 seconds.

Undertaker v Randy Orton

WRESTLEMANIA 21

This match is memorable as it was one of the very few occasions that 'the streak' was in jeopardy. Orton had emerged quickly on the WWE stage and he was helped on the night by his father, Bob Orton, who attacked Undertaker with his arm cast, leaving Orton Jnr to seize control of the match. He looked to have the contest well in his grasp, unleashing a Tombstone Piledriver of his own, before Undertaker hit back with one of his own to take his unbeaten record to 13/0.

Undertaker v Edge

WRESTLEMANIA XXIV

The main event of the night saw Edge putting his World Heavyweight Championship on the line and whatever Undertaker unleashed, his adversary was equal to. A trademark Tombstone Piledriver finally saw 'The Phenom' take control only for Curt Hawkins and Zack Ryder come to Edge's aid. A spear was applied to leave Undertaker facing a two-count but it was the quiet before the real storm. Both 'imposters' were quickly taken out, leaving Undertaker to administer a Hell's Gate submission hold on Edge. He became the new World Champion, extending his record to 16/0.

Undertaker v Kane

WRESTLEMANIA XX

Undertaker was accompanied to the ring by Paul Bearer, looking like the 'Deadman' of old, and again he took the upper hand against his brother by executing a Tombstone Piledriver and delivering a successful pinfall to make it undefeated with a 12/0 record. This was the second time that Kane faced Undertaker at *WrestleMania*, having previously lost at *WrestleMania* XIV.

THE MIZ® PROFILE

RAW

Height:	6-foot-1
Weight:	231 pounds
From:	Cleveland, OH
Signature Move:	Skull-crushing finale

Career Highlights:
WWE Champion; WWE Tag Team Champion; World Tag Team Champion; United States Champion; Unified Tag Team Champion

With the WWE Championship at stake, this was going to be no match for the faint hearted...

On one side of the ring we have John Cena, a vastly experienced campaigner in the heat of the *WrestleMania* battle, whereas on the other stands The Miz – yes, he is the reigning champ, with far less know-how of the greatest stage of all.

While he demands respect for his achievements, there's no doubting that The Awesome One has found himself involved in some controversy in his rise to

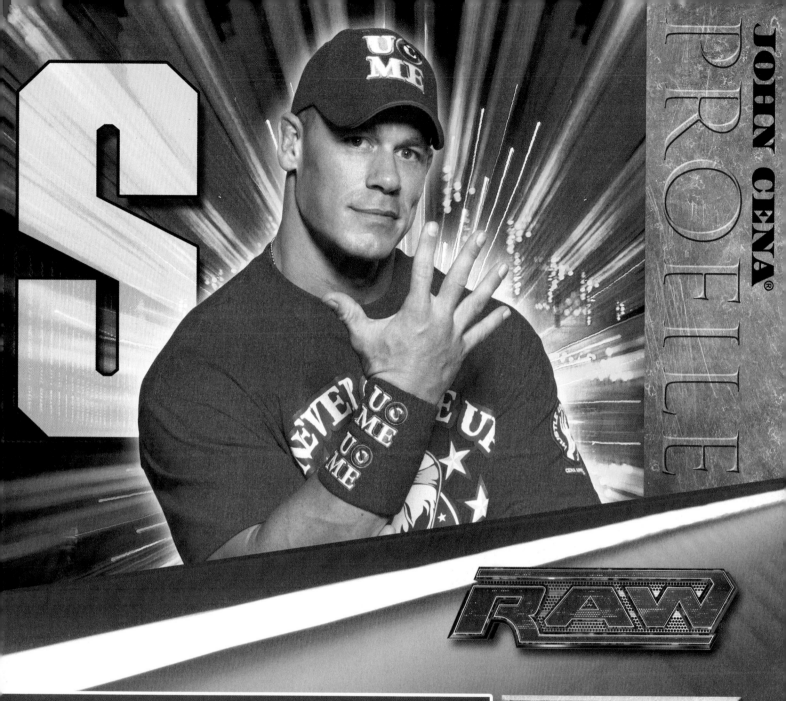

the top: cashing in his *Money in the Bank* contract on Randy Orton to seize the Championship... then he was heading for defeat in his title defence against Jerry Lawler only for some interference from Michael Cole to save the day...

Would he need some outside 'help' again to stop seven-time WWE Champion Cena who, after a spell on the sidelines, has hit back with a vengeance via the *Elimination Chamber* – namely Randy Orton, John Morrison, R-Truth, Sheamus and CM Punk – to find himself thrust right back in the spotlight.

Youth against experience – who will come out on top?

Height:	6-foot-1
Weight:	240 pounds
From:	West Newbury, MA
Signature Move:	Attitude Adjustment, & STF

Career Highlights:
World Heavyweight Champion;
WWE Champion; U.S. Champion;
World Tag Team Champion;
WWE Tag Team Champion;
2008 *Royal Rumble* Winner

"Introducing the champion, with Alex Riley in tow!"

"Cena means business in his new red T-shirt!"

"The Miz hits Cena with a clothesline – and gets a two count!"

"But Cena bounces back from the top rope!"

"He keeps up the attack with another charge at Cena!"

"To hit The Awesome One with a flying kick to the back of the neck!"

"The Miz sticks Cena into the turnbuckle to take control again!"

"And then follows up with a blow to the head!"

"Cena fights back with a shoulder tackle!"

"He then follows up with a Five Knuckle Shuffle!"

"But can't quite land an Attitude Adjustment!"

"It proves costly as he is met with a DDT and a two count!"

"It's another two count as The Miz tries a Neckbreaker!"

"Cena counters with the STF!"

"But The Miz somehow finds the rope and the hold is broken!"

"With the ref unaware, Alex Riley gives The Miz a helping hand!"

"He then gets the *Money in the Bank* briefcase to attack Cena!"

"But Cena is wise to the game!"

"Two versus one ain't fair. Now The Miz grabs the briefcase!"

"And delivers a huge blow on Cena's head!"

"Look, Miz has slid out of the ring!"

"Cena then delivers a clothesline!"

"But they are both out for the count over the barricade!"

"The referee counts ten and The Miz retains his title!"

"But look, The Rock has appeared ringside! And signals a re-start!"

"We're back on! Cena goes for another Attitude Adjustment!"

"But Rock wants more and he hits Cena with the Rock bottom!"

"Cena is counted out. It really is game over!"

"The Miz shows off his title. But then stares out The Rock!"

"The Rock is having none of it and attacks Miz with a Spinebuster!"

"Miz leaves with the title but his pride has taken a beating!"

PAGE 6-7 Who's the champ?
WWE Championship title – The Miz.
United States Championship title – Sheamus.
World Heavyweight Championship title – Edge.
Divas Championship – Eve.
Intercontinental Championship – Kofi Kingston.
Tag Team Championship – Heath Slater and Justin Gabriel.

PAGE 16 Wordsearch

I	A	I	N	A	M	E	L	T	S	E	R	W	N	H
M	R	O	E	X	J	G	N	W	J	D	E	A	T	H
Y	Q	E	F	P	V	C	A	P	L	D	P	E	V	B
D	E	A	T	H	V	A	L	L	E	Y	I	Q	B	U
X	V	J	W	G	R	E	D	M	C	I	D	T	R	R
V	R	E	J	P	G	N	J	K	W	R	N	O	H	I
C	F	J	H	I	T	A	P	R	U	U	S	M	E	E
A	G	E	V	Z	V	K	H	U	V	B	L	B	Q	D
S	L	E	A	H	C	I	M	N	W	A	H	S	R	A
K	D	T	Z	R	R	B	H	Z	I	W	X	T	S	L
E	E	P	J	A	Y	A	A	I	K	D	C	O	Z	I
T	L	R	E	R	A	E	B	L	U	A	P	N	P	V
W	A	L	T	U	O	T	S	A	L	T	L	E	H	E
M	A	L	S	E	K	O	H	C	H	G	D	X	M	N
S	Y	F	N	I	Q	W	I	G	U	S	M	A	M	V

PAGE 17 Crossword

PAGE 18-19 The Ultimate Nexus Quiz
1. Heath Slater
2. a
3. Mason Ryan
4. b
5. Bragging Rights
6. Burns
7. a. False b. False
8. Mason Ryan
9. a
10. a. Husky Harris b. David Otunga & c. CM Punk

PAGE 20-21 New to the Game
1. H 2. A 3. C 4. B 5. E 6. D 7. F 8. G.

PAGE 22-23 Hitting Top Gear!
1. Alberto Del Rio's knee pads & boots
2. Sheamus' cross
3. John Cena's armband
4. Jerry 'The King' Lawler's crown
5. Undertaker's hat
6. Drew McIntye's knee pads
7. Hornswoggle's suit
8. Big Show's off-the-shoulder suit

PAGE 24-27 What Do You Know?
1. John Morrison – Starship
2. CM Punk – Klutch
3. The Miz – Riley
4. Alberto Del Rio – Mexico
5. Edge – Spear
6. Big Show – Seven
7. John Cena – Heavyweight
8. Mark Henry – Strongest
9. Sheamus – Dublin
10. The Great Khali – India
11. Christian – Killswitch
12. Kane – Paul
13. Undertaker – Valley
14. Rey Mysterio – WrestleMania

PAGE 38 Mind the Gaps
Georgia, Holds, Rock, 19, Austin, Trish, Mask, Knee.

PAGE 39 Spot The Difference

PAGE 40-41 Hall Of Mirrors

1. Triple H
2. The Miz
3. John Morrison
4. The Great Khali
5. Big Show
6. Rey Mysterio
7. Undertaker
8. Hornswoggle

PAGE 42-43 The Ultimate Raw Quiz

1. **a.** R-Truth **b.** Sheamus **c.** John Morrison
2. John Morrison
3. John Cena
4. The King
5. b
6. c
7. True
8. Goldust
9. Triple H
10.

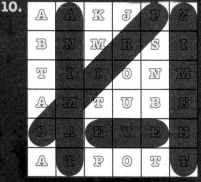

PAGE 44-45 Ladders Match Up

1. John Morrison
2. Dolph Ziggler

3. Christian
4. Jack Swagger
5. Sheamus
6. Kofi Kingston

PAGE 58-59 Old School Who?

1. Jim Duggan
2. Mr Perfect
3. British Bulldog
4. Stone Cold Steve Austin
5. Shawn Michaels
6. Booker T

PAGE 60-61 The Ultimate SmackDown Quiz

1. **a.** Kane **b.** Wade Barrett **c.** Jack Swagger
2. b
3. Hornswoggle
4. a
5. a – he is from Scotland, and not USA
6. Christian
7. False
8. Kofi Kingston
9. Mexico, 2010, Santino Marella,
10.

Q	R	T	R	J	A
B	N	H	F	T	G
E	E	P	R	G	A
G	N	P	A	U	L
D	A	L	Y	A	L
E	K	S	G	I	B

PAGE 62-63 Manic Maze

Ted DiBiase gets to go on holiday!

Page 64-65 Odd One Out

1. John Cena, the rest come from Europe
2. Theodore Long, the rest are commentators
3. Wade Barrett – the others have all won the World Heavyweight Championship
4. Kane – the others all weigh over 400lbs